THE SPEED OF LIGHT

To my Morecambe school pupils
who continue to inspire me.
— S. C.

To Chestnut, who purred through long nights
working on this book.
— W. T.

With thanks to Dr N. Baker-Campbell of the Department of Physics
and Dr Matthew Bothwell of the Institute of Astronomy at the
University of Cambridge for their contributions and advice.

First published 2025 by Nosy Crow Ltd
Wheat Wharf, 27a Shad Thames,
London, SE1 2XZ, UK

Nosy Crow Eireann Ltd
44 Orchard Grove, Kenmare,
Co Kerry, V93 FY22, Ireland

ISBN 978 1 80513 315 5 (HB)
ISBN 978 1 80513 316 2 (PB)

Nosy Crow and associated logos are trademarks
and/or registered trademarks of Nosy Crow Ltd.

Text © Simon Chapman 2025
Illustrations © Wenjia Tang 2025

Published in collaboration with the University of Cambridge

The right of Simon Chapman to be identified as the author
and Wenjia Tang to be identified as the illustrator
of this work has been asserted.
All rights reserved.

This book is sold subject to the condition that it shall not,
by way of trade or otherwise, be lent, hired out or otherwise circulated
in any form of binding or cover other than that in which it is published.
No part of this publication may be reproduced, stored in a retrieval system,
or transmitted in any form or by any means (electronic, mechanical, photocopying,
recording or otherwise) without the prior written permission of Nosy Crow Ltd.

The publisher and copyright holders prohibit the use of
either text or illustrations to develop any generative machine learning
artificial intelligence (AI) models or related technologies.

A CIP catalogue record for this book is available from the British Library.

Printed in Poland following rigorous ethical sourcing standards.

10 9 8 7 6 5 4 3 2 1 (HB)
10 9 8 7 6 5 4 3 2 1 (PB)

THE SPEED OF LIGHT

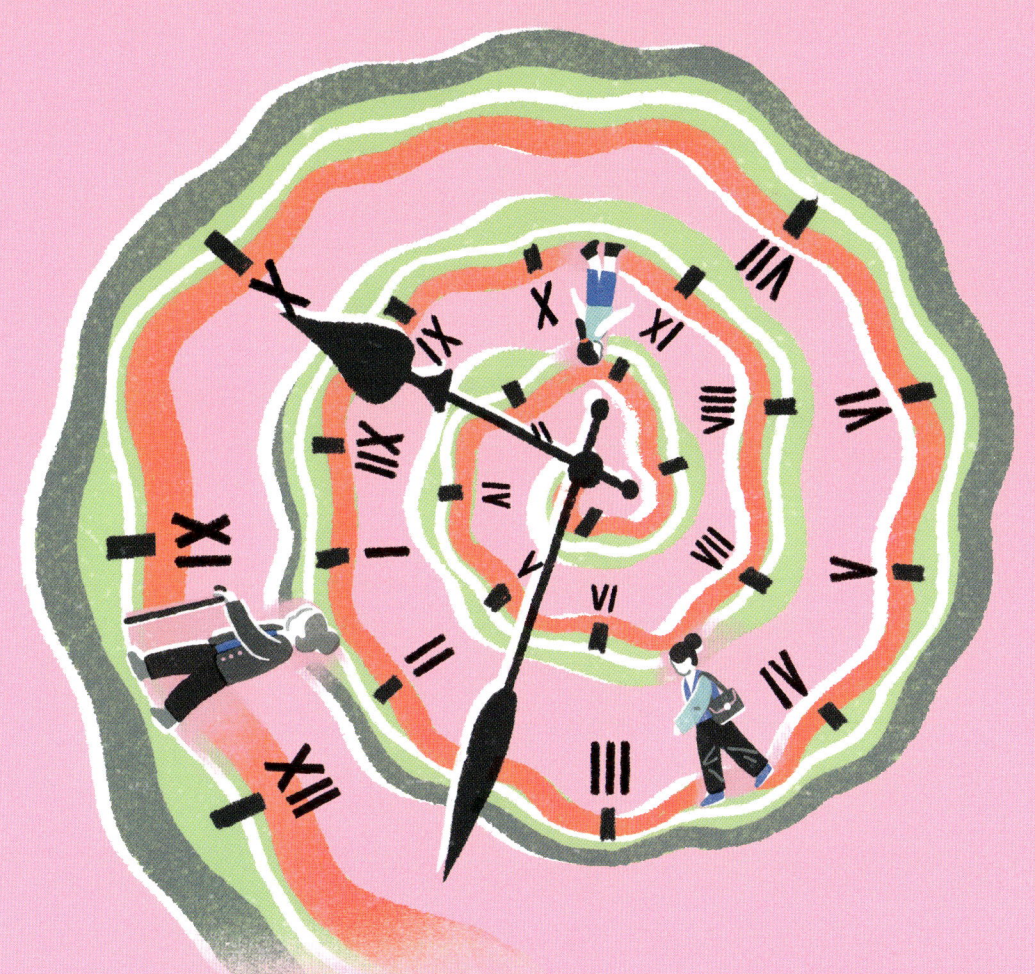

written by
SIMON CHAPMAN

illustrated by
WENJIA TANG

Contents

Who was Albert Einstein?
Pages 6-7

How fast is light?
Pages 8-9

Are you sitting still?
Pages 10-11

How can we show relativity in action?
Pages 12-13

How do we use relativity in real life?
Pages 14-15

How can speed change the sounds we hear?
Pages 16-17

What colour are the stars?
Pages 18-19

What would happen if we could travel at the speed of light?
Pages 20-21

How can time stretch?
Pages 22-23

What is spacetime?
Pages 24-25

What can we learn from smashing atoms?
Pages 26-27

Can anything travel faster than light?
Pages 28-29

Glossary and Index
Pages 30-32

Introduction

You press the light switch and instantly the room is bright. It is as if the light coming from the bulb took no time at all to get to you. But it did take time. It's just that light travels incredibly fast. What's more, as things travel close to the speed of light, strange things happen. Objects become heavier. Distances get squashed. Time stretches out.

These ideas are incredibly complex and yet, remarkably, they were all thought up by just one scientist over 100 years ago: Albert Einstein. He called these ideas his theory of relativity.

With every advance in technology since, from sending people into space to building huge machines to smash particles together at close to the speed of light, we are finding out that the things Einstein said keep proving to be true.

—SIMON CHAPMAN

Who was Albert Einstein?

Albert Einstein is probably the most important physicist of the twentieth century. He was the first scientist to come up with an explanation for how stars change the gas they are made of into pure energy, and he developed the quantum physics that led to solar panels which use the power of the Sun.

But his biggest idea was his **theory of relativity**. Einstein's theory contained a lot of incredible ideas about the behaviour of light, **gravity** and space. He said that as objects approach the **speed of light**, distances squash and time itself stretches.

If this sounds strange to you, you are not alone! When Einstein published his mind-bending theories, many other scientists did not believe them. But again and again, they have been proved to be correct.

Einstein's theory of relativity involves complicated ideas that are hard to understand all at once. But break it down into smaller parts, and you will soon get a better idea of how Einstein's ideas have shaped how we see the universe.

THE LIFE OF EINSTEIN

1879 Born in Ulm, Germany. Einstein's father runs an electrical company and his mother is a keen musician. As an adult, Einstein loves playing the violin. Einstein does well at school but annoys his teachers by always questioning their ideas.

1896 Fails the exam to attend a research university in Zurich, Switzerland, but is let in anyway because his maths scores are so high.

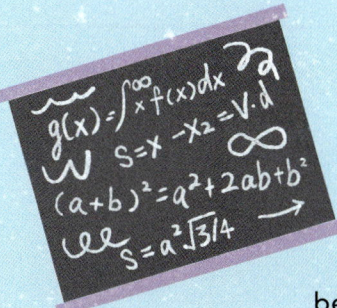

1902 Works in the patent office in Bern, Switzerland. The office looked at new inventions to check they were original ideas. While working here, Einstein daydreams 'thought experiments' which lead to his theories on space and time.

1915 Einstein's wonder year. He writes up his ideas and becomes famous.

1921 Einstein wins the Nobel Prize for Physics.

1930 Einstein moves to the United States and starts working at Princeton University, New Jersey.

1955 Einstein dies aged 76, and his brain is preserved for science. Surprisingly, it is slightly below average size.

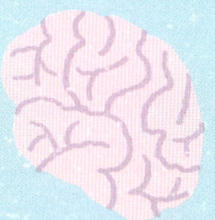

7

How fast is light?

To begin to understand the theory of relativity, first, we need to comprehend the speed of light. It's not just fast, it's SO fast that it's hard to even imagine.

Let's compare it to things you might be more familiar with. How far can people, animals and machines move in one second?

Saturn V rocket
2,760 metres

Peregrine falcon diving
83 metres

Person walking
1.3 metres

Olympic sprinter
12.4 metres

Horse galloping
14 metres

X15 rocket plane
2,020 metres

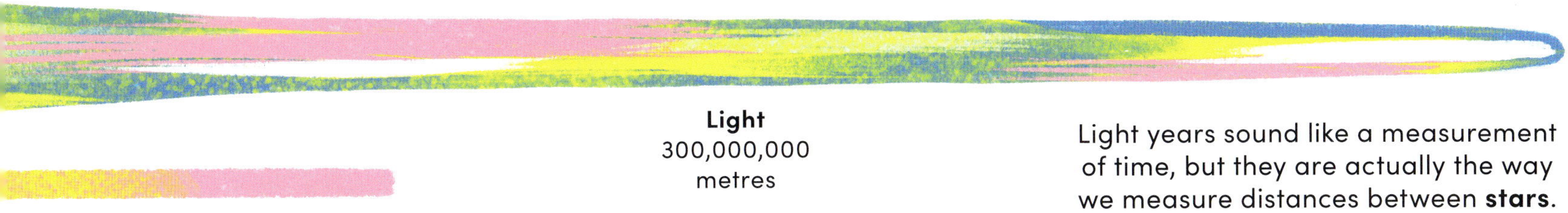

NOTHING FASTER THAN LIGHT

Light travels 300,000,000 metres every second through air and space. Nothing in the universe is faster. What's more, light does not get tired and slow down like cheetahs, human sprinters and horses. It does not run out of fuel like cars, planes and rockets. Light travels at this speed forever.

Light
300,000,000 metres

Light years sound like a measurement of time, but they are actually the way we measure distances between **stars**. A light year is equal to the distance light travels in one Earth year, which is about 9.5 trillion kilometres.

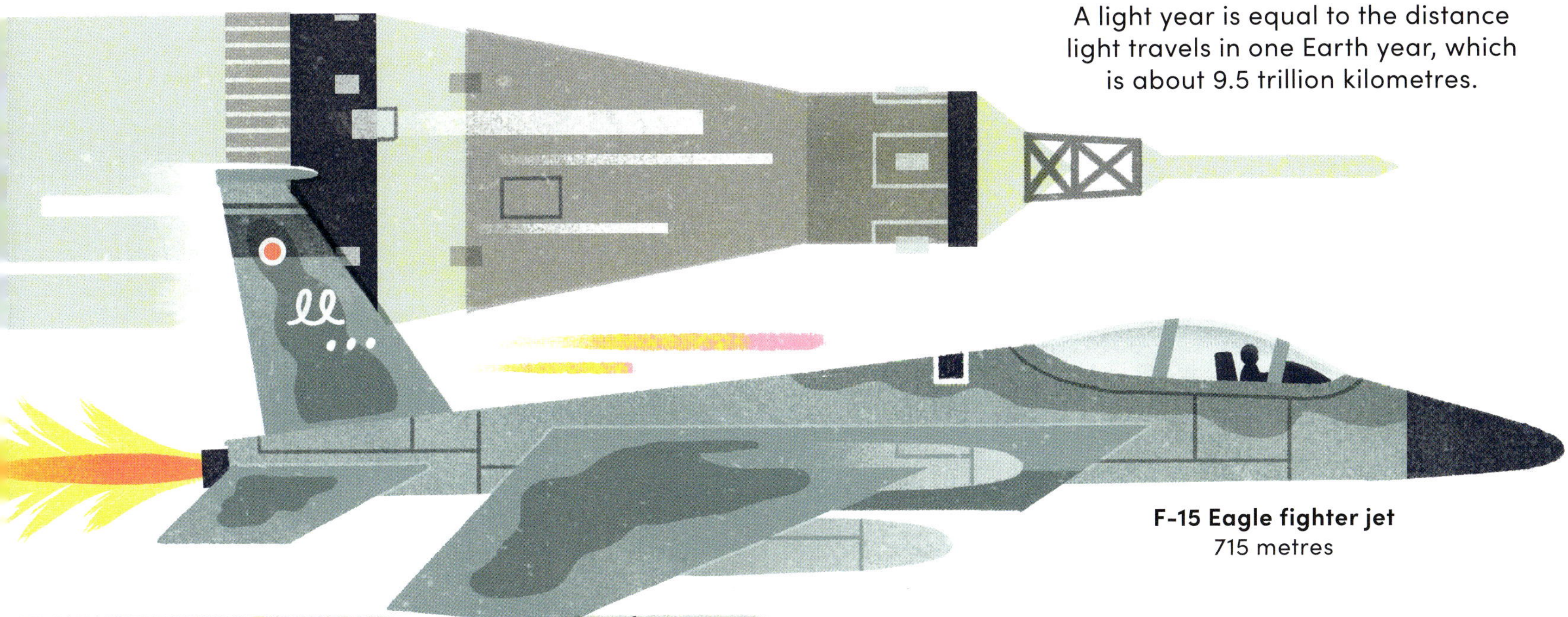

F-15 Eagle fighter jet
715 metres

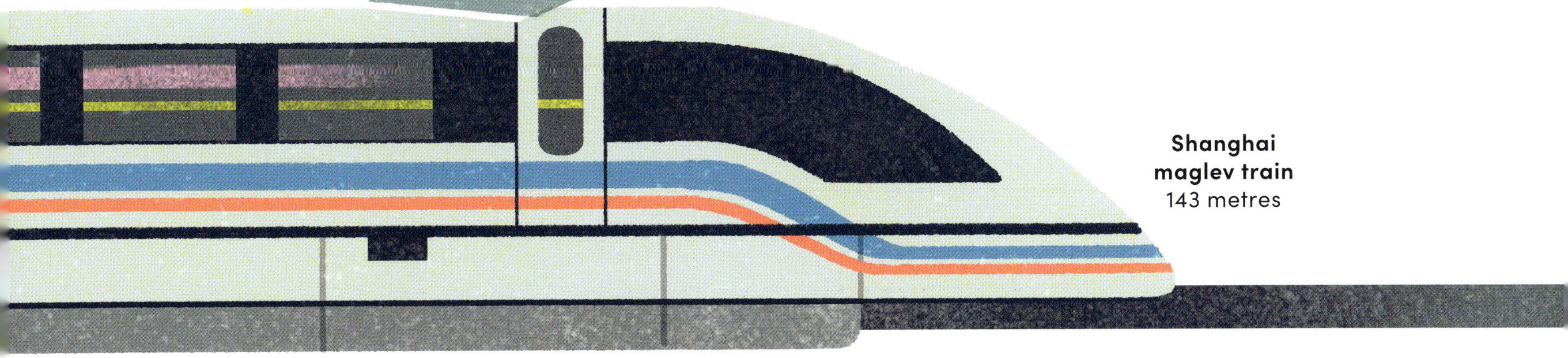

Shanghai maglev train
143 metres

Cheetah sprinting
29 metres

Formula One racing car
100 metres

Are you sitting still?

Next, we need to try and wrap our heads around the idea of relativity. Einstein tested his ideas through daydreams, which he called thought experiments.

Here's an example you can try...

THINK LIKE EINSTEIN: The Moving Chair

IS YOUR CHAIR MOVING?

IS YOUR ROOM MOVING?

IS YOUR HOUSE OR SCHOOL MOVING?

From your point of view, everything stays just where it is. But Earth is turning on its axis (an invisible line that goes through the centre of the planet). It takes one day (24 hours) to spin around once. So, while you appear to be sitting still, you are actually moving at 460 metres per second.

Added to that, the Earth orbits (goes around) the **Sun** every year.

For that matter, the Sun is one of millions of **stars** in our **galaxy**, all moving around the galactic centre.

Our galaxy is moving too. It is one of millions of galaxies that make up the **universe**.

SO, ARE YOU REALLY SITTING STILL? NO!

You are moving incredibly quickly. However, everything else around you is moving at the same speed, which is why you don't feel like you are on a never-ending rollercoaster.

This is **relativity**: how fast something appears to be moving depends on what you are comparing it to.

In other words, you might feel like you are moving slowly or not at all, but to an outside observer (for example, an alien watching Earth from deep space) you are moving extremely fast.

How can we show relativity in action?

There are lots of easy ways we can prove that the measurement of movement depends on the relative speed and position of the observer.

THINK LIKE EINSTEIN: Train Ride in the Dark

1. Imagine you are on a train, passing trees and houses and platforms.

If the ride is smooth with no jolting and the train stays at the same speed, it might feel like you are not moving at all.

2. But what does someone outside the train see? To them it looks like you are zooming along at top speed.

3. Now, imagine the lights go out on the train, and someone hands you a glowing ball. You throw the ball up in the air, then catch it. Up, then down. Up, then down. From your point of view inside the train, the ball is moving up and down but not forwards.

4. However, go back to the observer outside. From their point of view, the ball appears to be bouncing along the track, up and down and forwards. This proves the speed and direction of the ball is **relative** to the observer.

EINSTEIN'S JOURNEY

Einstein would have seen **relative motion** in action as he travelled by tram to work at the Bern patent office. The tram would whizz past pedestrians, while cars and horse carriages travelling at the same speed and in the same direction as his tram would appear still from his point of view.

How do we use relativity in real life?

Have you ever seen a movie where bank robbers throw bags of money from their getaway car to their friends in a van next to them? Or car chase scenes where action heroes jump onto the bad guys' car?

It's not as unrealistic as you might think!

For this to work, both the van and the car must be travelling at exactly the same speed in the same direction. To someone in the van or someone in the car, the other vehicle would look like it isn't moving. The people in the car could easily step across into the van. (Of course, if they looked down and saw the ground speeding past underneath, they might be too scared to move!)

REFUELLING ON THE GO!

In real life, scientists and engineers have come up with lots of practical ways to use **relative motion**. Some helicopters and military planes can be refuelled mid-air, without needing to land.

To do this, both the aircraft needing fuel and the aircraft carrying fuel need to fly close to each other at the same speed and in the same direction.

TRAINS THAT NEVER STOP

Transport designers are also thinking about using the idea of **relativity** to make super-fast train systems, where a train could travel around a whole country without ever slowing down or stopping.

To board the super-fast train, passengers would first get onto another train at their local station. This second train would speed up next to the non-stopping train. When both trains were at the same speed, passengers could step across as if both trains were still. Anybody who wanted to get off the non-stopping train would get onto the other train, which would then slow to a stop at the next station.

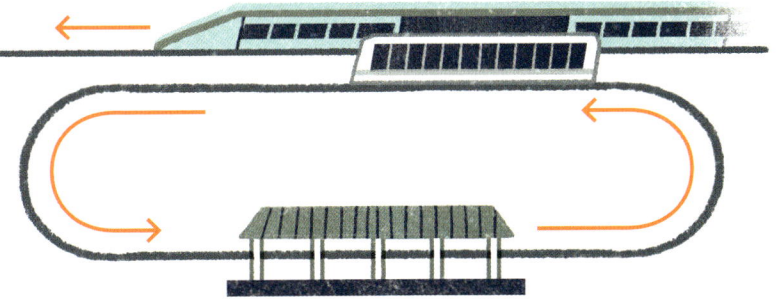

How can speed change the sounds we hear?

Science isn't just in books, it's all around you! For instance, even if you haven't heard of the Doppler effect, you will definitely have heard it in action.

HOW DO WE HEAR?

Sound is caused by objects vibrating (moving backwards and forwards very fast). The vibrations travel in waves from the object, through the air, until they reach our ears. The more squashed together the waves of vibration are, the higher **pitched** the sound.

A whistle makes a high-pitched sound:

A double bass makes a low-pitched sound:

The distance between two dips or two peaks is called a **wavelength**.

THE DOPPLER EFFECT

Have you ever listened to a fire engine's siren as it rushes past you?

NE-NAW NE-NAW NEE NAWWW...

You also might have noticed something like this when a fast car races past.

EEE-OW!

When the fire engine is driving towards you, the sound waves from its siren become squashed together as they arrive where you are more often and the pitch your ears hear is higher.

As the fire engine zooms away, the opposite happens. As the distance between where you are standing and the fire engine increases, the sound waves become stretched as they arrive where you are less often and the pitch your ears hear is lower.

Sound waves travel about a million times slower than light waves.

This change of wavelength is called the **Doppler effect**.

Light travels as waves too, although in a different way to sound. The Doppler effect also works with light waves, but when these are squashed or stretched, it is the colour of the light we see that changes.

What colour are the stars?

This might seem like a simple question, but there is a lot more to it than you might imagine!

Light is made up of all the colours in the rainbow. When light waves hit an object, some of the light is absorbed by the object, and some is reflected into our eyes.

Certain objects reflect light with a longer **wavelength** (which appears red), while others reflect light with a shorter wavelength (which appears blue or purple).

red   orange   yellow   green   blue   indigo   violet

THINK LIKE EINSTEIN: Rocket Trip

Imagine you are in a rocket speeding away from the **Sun**, towards another **star**.

As the rocket travels rapidly away from the Sun, the Sun's light waves reach it less often, and from your position in the rocket, the light waves will appear stretched out to a longer wavelength. From your point of view, the Sun's light will look orange or red. We call this **red-shift**.

Now turn your attention to the new star ahead. As the rocket approaches, the light waves appear squashed together, as if the light has a shorter wavelength. The light from the star in front will look green, blue or even violet, if your rocket is moving towards it fast enough. This is called **blue-shift**.

The light from nearly every **galaxy** we can see in the night sky has red-shifted. This tells astronomers that the galaxies are all moving away from the Earth. The **universe** is getting bigger.

WHAT ABOUT ANDROMEDA?

The light from the Andromeda galaxy is blue-shifted. Andromeda contains a trillion stars hurtling towards our own Milky Way galaxy, but it will not reach us for another 4.5 billion years. When it does, there will be no crash. The space between the stars is so huge that the two galaxies will just merge together.

What would happen if we could travel at the speed of light?

Nothing in the universe travels faster than light. But we can imagine what we would see if we could travel at light speed.

THINK LIKE EINSTEIN: Speedy Spaceship

Imagine that you are a passenger in a stationary car. It is raining and drops are falling straight down. However, once the car starts moving, you can see the rain hitting the windscreen at an angle, even though you know it is still falling straight down.

Now, instead of a car, imagine you are in a spaceship floating in space. Instead of raindrops, the light rays from a nearby **star** reach all sides of the spaceship.

Back to the car. As you speed up even more, the rain starts hitting the windscreen almost straight on. No raindrops reach the back of the car.

Back in space on your imaginary ship, you speed up to close to the **speed of light**. Now, the light rays are hitting the spaceship head on and, just like the raindrops on the speeding car, no light rays reach the back of the ship.

As a result, everything ahead of the spaceship looks incredibly bright. Everything behind appears black.

EVERYTHING LOOKS SQUASHED!

If you think that is weird, things would get even stranger as the spaceship got even closer to the speed of light. To you and its crew, everything ahead would look shortened, including distances.

And if anyone was watching the spaceship pass by, the spaceship itself would look squashed, like a balloon squished out of shape. At the speed of light, it would look squashed flat.

How can time stretch?

When Einstein took the tram home from his work at the patent office, he would look at a clocktower out of the window and wonder what he would see if he were travelling at the speed of light.

You might think that time is the one thing you can rely on. A minute is always a minute, and an hour is always an hour. But at extremely high speeds, Einstein believed that time would slow down.

THINK LIKE EINSTEIN: Twins in Time

Imagine you have a pair of twins. You put one on a very speedy spaceship, which travels close to the **speed of light**, while one remains on Earth.

From each of the twins' points of view, time would appear to pass normally.

LESS TIME PASSES WHEN YOU MOVE FAST

In 1971, scientists finally tested Einstein's idea that speed could affect time. They put accurate **atomic clocks** on airplanes and flew them around the world. When the planes landed, they compared the times on their clocks with the time on another identical clock left standing still in their laboratory.

The times were different. A fraction less time had passed on the planes than had passed back on the ground. Once again, Einstein's **theory** was correct.

As the atomic clocks used airline passenger seats, the scientists had to buy them tickets. The name on the tickets was 'Mr Clock'.

After flying for two weeks, the astronaut twin returns to Earth to discover that their twin looks much older than when they left.

For the twin on Earth, years have passed, not weeks! Einstein called this effect **time dilation**.

What is spacetime?

We live our lives in three dimensions. Everything has a length, a width and a height. Einstein believed there is a fourth dimension too – *time* – and that it does not always have to move forwards. He thought that gravity, like speed, could affect time and called this idea spacetime.

WHAT IS GRAVITY?

Gravity acts like an invisible force that pulls objects towards each other. The bigger an object's **mass** (the amount of 'stuff' it is made of), the stronger its gravitational pull. We are pulled towards the Earth because it has a huge mass. Einstein worked out that gravity was actually caused by **spacetime** being bent!

GRAVITY BENDING LIGHT

Einstein believed that the mass of large **stars** could dent spacetime so much that they would bend light too. An astronomer called Arthur Eddington proved this in 1919 during an eclipse when the Moon came between the Earth and the **Sun**, blocking the Sun's light. Several stars close to the shaded-out Sun appeared slightly out of place. The Sun's mass had bent their light around.

THINK LIKE EINSTEIN: Space Trampoline

Imagine space – or spacetime – as a stretchy rubber trampoline, and a massive star (with an extremely heavy mass) as a bowling ball. When the bowling ball is placed on the trampoline, it sinks down and creates a dent.

In the same way, the mass of a big star causes spacetime to curve, creating gravity.

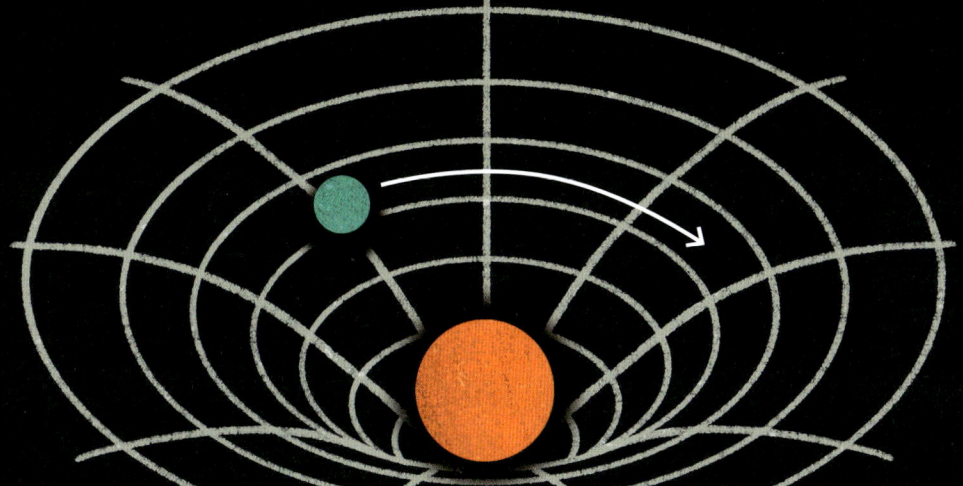

Now imagine the planets as marbles. If you roll a marble onto the trampoline with enough force, it will roll in circles around the dent created by the bowling ball.

This shows us exactly what happens in space: a planet orbiting around a star is following the curve in spacetime that the star has created.

WHAT IS A BLACK HOLE?

Black holes are what is left behind when massive stars explode. They are deep — possibly bottomless — wells with an incredibly heavy mass squashed down to an incredibly tiny size.

Their gravity is so powerful that not even light can escape.

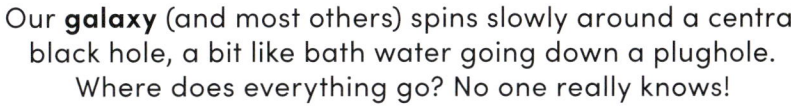

Our **galaxy** (and most others) spins slowly around a central black hole, a bit like bath water going down a plughole. Where does everything go? No one really knows!

25

What can we learn from smashing atoms?

Atoms are the building blocks that make up all the matter in the universe. They are extremely small, and made up of even smaller particles called electrons, protons and neutrons.

In the Large Hadron Collider in Geneva, Switzerland, scientists are trying to find out what matter is made of. They accelerate protons to nearly the **speed of light**, then smash them into each other to see what pieces are left over.

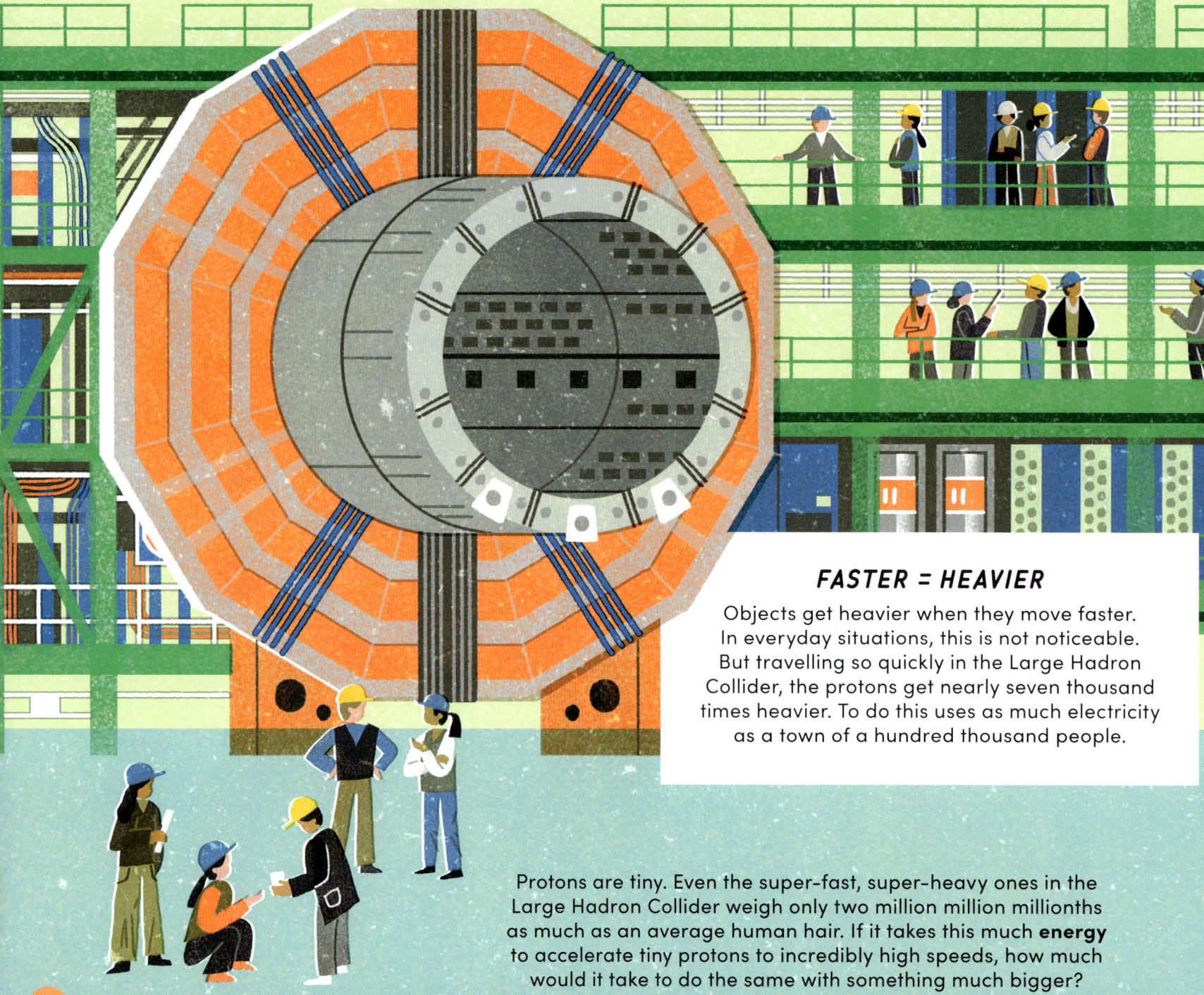

FASTER = HEAVIER
Objects get heavier when they move faster. In everyday situations, this is not noticeable. But travelling so quickly in the Large Hadron Collider, the protons get nearly seven thousand times heavier. To do this uses as much electricity as a town of a hundred thousand people.

Protons are tiny. Even the super-fast, super-heavy ones in the Large Hadron Collider weigh only two million million millionths as much as an average human hair. If it takes this much **energy** to accelerate tiny protons to incredibly high speeds, how much would it take to do the same with something much bigger?

$E = mc^2$

To answer this question, Einstein came up with the equation $E=mc^2$. E stands for Energy, m stands for mass, and c stands for the speed of light. So, the equation means: Energy = mass x (speed of light x speed of light). In other words, matter can change into energy and energy can change into matter.

There are many examples of $E=mc^2$ in real life. For example, in nuclear power plants, certain metals such as uranium are turned into energy that is used to power homes and schools.

THINK LIKE EINSTEIN: The Heavy Ship

Infinity is the biggest number possible, a number that goes on and on and on without end.

If we accept that objects get heavier the faster they move, a spaceship moving at light speed would be infinitely heavy. It would need an infinite amount of energy to get it to move that fast . . . and to make that energy we would need an infinite amount of matter, more than exists in the whole **universe**.

Under these conditions, do you think reaching light speed could ever be possible?

Can anything travel faster than light?

Einstein believed reaching the speed of light was impossible. But what if it isn't?

ARE WARP DRIVES POSSIBLE?

It *might* be possible for a little bit of space to travel faster than light. Engineers could potentially build something called a **warp drive** that bends **spacetime** into a bubble around a spaceship. This bubble would move faster than light, transporting the spaceship across vast distances.

Right now, warp drives are the stuff of science fiction books and movies. But who knows? One day, they might be possible.

F.T.L? (FASTER THAN LIGHT?)

Some scientists believe there might be special particles called **tachyons** that have no **mass** and therefore could travel faster than light. Einstein's **theory of relativity** says they are possible, but so far, no one has found them.

Einstein's theory of relativity also states that as objects get faster, time for them slows down. So, if tachyons do exist, does that mean time travel is possible? What would happen if a person could travel faster than light? Would time stop, or run backwards?

THINK LIKE EINSTEIN: Time Traveller Trouble

If you could go back in time, could you change the past? What if you did something that stopped the future you from being born? What would happen to the 'you' in the past?

That last famous question is known as the **grandfather paradox** and is one that scientists have been wrestling with ever since Einstein came up with his theories of relativity and **time dilation**.

NOW, IT'S YOUR TURN!

We still have so much to learn about the universe and how it works. Perhaps something you imagine one day, as a daydream or a thought experiment, will continue to further our understanding of science and change the future of our world. As Einstein said:

"LEARN FROM YESTERDAY, LIVE FOR TODAY, HOPE FOR TOMORROW. THE IMPORTANT THING IS NOT TO STOP QUESTIONING."

Glossary

Atoms

The tiny particles that all things are made of.

Atomic clock

A very accurate clock that measures time by how quickly certain atoms vibrate.

Black hole

A collapsed star that has so much gravity that light cannot escape.

Blue-shift

When light waves given out by a star or galaxy moving towards you are squashed together because of the Doppler effect.

Doppler effect

How waves given out by a moving object appear stretched out if the object is moving away or squashed closer if the object is moving closer.

Energy

What makes things work, move and change.

Galaxy

A collection of hundreds of thousands to millions of stars, gas and dust.

Gravity

The attraction between massive objects, caused by the bending of space and time.

Mass

How much 'stuff' something is made of.

Pitch (of a sound)

How high or low a note is.

Quantum physics

The study of tiny particles, including protons, electrons and atoms.

Red-shift

When light waves given out by a star or galaxy moving away are stretched longer because of the Doppler effect.

Relativity

The idea that objects appear different depending on how fast they are moving compared with other objects.

Relative motion

The movement of one object compared to another. For example, two cars moving side by side in the same direction at 30 kilometres per hour would have a speed of 0 km/h (30 - 30) compared to each other. If they were moving in opposite directions, their speed relative to each other would be 60 km/h (30 + 30).

Space time

The idea that when scientists think about space, they have to consider time as well as distances.

Speed of light

300,000,000 metres per second in space. The fastest speed possible.

Star

A giant ball of hydrogen gas that gives out energy because its enormous force of gravity squashes its atoms together (nuclear fusion).

Sun

A medium-sized yellow star around which the Earth revolves.

Tachyon

A theoretical particle that can travel faster than light.

Time dilation

Time stretching when objects travel close to the speed of light.

Theory

An idea that scientists can put to the test.

Warp drive

An idea that may be possible in the future to make spaceships travel faster than light.

Universe

All the planets, stars, galaxies. Everything!

Wavelength

The distance for a complete wave, which is the peak of one wave to the next.

Index

A
Andromeda galaxy   19
Astronauts   23
Atomic clock   23
Atoms   26

B
Black holes   25
Blue-shift   19

C
Cars   9, 13, 14, 17, 20-21

D
Doppler effect   16-17

E
Earth   9, 10-11, 19, 22-23, 24
Eclipse   24
Einstein, Albert   5, 6-7, 10, 12-13, 19, 22-23, 24-25, 27, 28-29
Electricity   26
Electrons   26
Engineers   15, 28

G
Galaxies   11, 19, 25
   see also Andromeda
grandfather paradox, the   29
Gravity   6, 24-25

H
Helicopters   15

L
Large Hadron Collider   26
Light   5, 6, 8-9, 13, 17, 18-19, 20-21, 22, 24-25, 26-27, 28
Light years   9

M
Mass   24-25, 27-28
Matter   26-27
Moon   24

N
Neutrons   26

P
Planes   9, 15, 23
Planets   9, 10-11, 19, 22-23, 24-25
Protons   26

R
Red-shift   19
Relativity   5, 6-7, 8, 10-11, 12-13, 14-15, 28-29
Rocket   8-9, 19

S
Scientists   5, 6-7, 15, 23, 26, 28-29
Sound   16-17
Space   5, 6-7, 9, 11, 19, 20-21, 24-25, 28-29
Spaceship   20-21, 22, 27, 28
Spacetime   24-25, 28
Speed of light   5, 6, 8, 20-21, 22, 26-27, 28
Stars   6, 9, 11, 18-19, 20, 24-25
Sun   6, 10-11, 19, 24

T
Time   5, 6-7, 9, 22-23, 24-25, 28-29
Time travel   28-29
Trains   9, 12-13, 15

U
Universe   7, 9, 11, 19, 20, 26-27, 29
Uranium   27

W
Warp drives   28
Wavelength   16-17, 18-19